SOCCER

BY CHRÖS McDOUGALL

CONTENT CONSULTANT
ROGER ALLAWAY, US SOCCER HISTORIAN

Published by ABDO Publishing Company, PO Box 398166, Minneapolis, MN 55439. Copyright © 2012 by Abdo Consulting Group, Inc. International copyrights reserved in all countries. No part of this book may be reproduced in any form without written permission from the publisher. SportsZone™ is a trademark and logo of ABDO Publishing Company.

Printed in the United States of America,
North Mankato, Minnesota
102011
012012

Editor: Holly Saari
Copy Editor: Chelsey Whitcomb
Series Design and Cover Production: Craig Hinton
Interior Production: Marie Tupy

Photo Credits: Rebecca Blackwell/AP Images, cover (bottom); Rafal Olkis/iStockphoto, cover (top); Sean Dempsey/AP Images, 1; Ariel Schalit/AP Images, 5; Issouf Sanogo/AFP/Getty Images, 9; Fabian Bimmer/AP Images, 11; Rebecca Blackwell/AP Images, 13; Bob Thomas/Popperfoto/Getty Images, 15, 58 (top); Bob Thomas/Popperfoto/Getty Images, 19; AP Images, 21; Popperfoto/Getty Images, 23, 58 (middle); AP Images, 25; AP Images, 27; AP Images, 29; AP Images, 31; AP Images, 33; STF/AFP/Getty Images, 35, 58 (bottom); Carlo Fumagalli/AP Images, 39, 59 (top); Mark Lennihan/AP Images, 41; Eric Draper/AP Images, 43; John T. Greilick/AP Images, 47; Lacy Atkins/AP Images, 49, 59 (middle); Darryl Dyck/AP Images, 51; Andres Kudacki/AP Images, 54; Michael Probst/AP Images, 57, 59 (bottom)

Library of Congress Cataloging-in-Publication Data
McDougall, Chrös
  Soccer / by Chrös McDougall.
    p. cm. -- (Best sport ever)
  Includes index.
  ISBN 978-1-61783-146-1
  1. Soccer--Juvenile literature. I. Title.
  GV943.25.M33 2012
  796.334--dc23
                    2011034601

UNITED

Côte d'Ivoire, or Ivory Coast, has long been a source of pride in Africa. The West African nation was one of the continent's most stable countries. It was known for providing the world with cocoa, coffee, and other crops. Then, at the dawn of the twenty-first century, Ivory Coast became known for something else: soccer.

A new generation of Ivorian players emerged. The best players began showing up in the world's top professional leagues, such as the English Premier League (EPL) and France's Ligue 1. Perhaps the greatest player was forward Didier Drogba. In 2004, he joined EPL team Chelsea Football Club, whose last league title had been in the 1954–55 season. The team won back-to-back titles in Drogba's first two seasons.

Didier Drogba is one of the best soccer players to come from Ivory Coast.

Country in Crisis

Not all was well for the Ivorian players, however. Back home, their nation had split into civil war. The northern part of Ivory Coast was mostly Muslim, and the southern part of the country was mostly Christian. The two sides disagreed over many issues. In 2002, rebels took control of the north and went to war against the government-controlled south.

The religious tension threatened to split the country in two. Even the country's soccer stars were on different sides of the conflict. Drogba was a Christian from the southern part of the country. Other Ivorian soccer stars, such as brothers Kolo Touré and Yaya Touré, were Muslims from the north.

Those players spent most of the year playing for their respective professional teams around the world. But a few times each year they also came together to form Ivory Coast's national team, which played other national teams.

FAN MEMBERSHIP

Many soccer teams around the world are sporting clubs that offer paid fan membership and occasionally have multiple sports teams. For FC Barcelona in Spain, fans who buy into the club get access to tickets and vote to elect a new team president. A similar system exists within Seattle Sounders FC in the United States.

The Ivorian national team was a mix of players of different religious and ethnic backgrounds. But the players knew they represented the entire Ivory Coast, not just certain parts. As Drogba said, "In the national team, we are all brothers."

To the World Cup

Amid their country's unrest, the Ivorian players began working toward a new goal during the summer of 2005: qualifying for the 2006 World Cup. The players knew that fans from all parts of the country were following them. They knew the Ivorian people could use a positive distraction from the fighting. The national team, known as the Elephants, wanted to prove that Ivorians could work together to achieve great things.

Qualifying for the World Cup would not be easy, though. The tournament, which is held every four years, began in 1930 as a global soccer championship. Yet Ivory Coast had never qualified. In 2005, Ivory Coast had one of the best teams in Africa. However, to qualify, the Elephants had to win their qualifying group. Each team in the six-team qualifying group would play each other twice, once at home and once on the road. That meant Ivory Coast would have to finish ahead of African powers Cameroon and Egypt, who were in its group.

The Elephants got off to a good start. Fans from around the country celebrated in the streets after each win. And following each game, Drogba led the team in prayer. They prayed in both Christian and Muslim verses.

Fans lost some hope when the Elephants lost their second-to-last game in the tournament. That meant they would have to win their final game and hope Cameroon lost its final game. But that is exactly what happened on October 8, 2005. Ivory Coast had qualified for its first World Cup.

As fans around the country celebrated, Drogba spoke to a television reporter: "Ivorians, men and women, from the north and the south, the center and the west, you've seen this," Drogba said with his teammates gathered around him. "We've proven to you that the people of Côte d'Ivoire can all live together side

MORE THAN A JOG

Soccer games consist of two 45-minute halves with a few additional minutes of injury time added to them. With only three substitutions allowed per team, the players get quite a workout. In 2007, television broadcasts began tracking approximately how far a given player had run in the game. Gennaro Gattuso, a midfielder for AC Milan in Italy, is known as one of the hardest-working players in soccer. In one 2007 game, he was tracked at running more than 10 kilometers (6.2 miles)—and he was substituted out in the 85th minute.

Didier Drogba, *top*, and his Ivory Coast teammates celebrate after beating
Benin in a qualifying match for the 2006 World Cup.

by side, play together towards one same goal: qualifying for the World Cup." He finished his speech with an appeal for peace: "The only country in Africa with wealth cannot sink into war like this. Please, put down your weapons, organize elections and things will get better."

The players' example and Drogba's plea had an effect on their countrymen. Amid the days-long celebration, the government and rebel leaders called for peace. Thanks to the Elephants, the country would be one—at least temporarily—as it cheered on the team at the World Cup in Germany.

The World Cup did not go as hoped, though. The Elephants were drawn into a challenging group that included Argentina and the Netherlands. Only the top two teams in each group

SOCCER STOPS WARS

The 2006 World Cup was not the only time that soccer has temporarily stopped a war. In 1915, England and Germany were fighting against each other in World War I. However, the two sides called a truce for Christmas Day, and some of the enemy soldiers played soccer together.

In 1967, the West African nation of Nigeria was immersed in a civil war when Brazilian superstar Pelé came for an exhibition game. A two-day cease-fire was called so all Nigerians would have an opportunity to watch in peace as Pelé played.

The Ivory Coast's Didier Zokora, *right*, congratulates Didier Drogba after Drogba scored a goal against Argentina in the 2006 World Cup.

advance to the second round. Ivory Coast finished third. Although they left the tournament empty-handed, the Elephants had helped begin their country's road to reconciliation. But there was still much work to be done.

Uniting Power

In 2007, Drogba was named the African Player of the Year. He celebrated in Abidjan, Ivory Coast's capital. But he wanted to celebrate with the whole nation rather than just the southern part. He asked President Laurent Gbagbo if the Elephants could play their next game in Bouaké, the capital of the rebel-held north. The president agreed.

The fans were in a frenzy when the Elephants arrived. People cried out in joy when they saw Drogba and the Elephants. The team represented peace. Drogba scored the fifth goal in the 5–0 win over Madagascar. The next day, a front-page headline in an Abidjan newspaper declared: FIVE GOALS TO ERASE FIVE YEARS OF WAR.

Drogba and the Elephants did not bring an end to Ivory Coast's problems. Although there has been progress, the sides are still searching for solutions. But the

SOCCER VIOLENCE

Through the years, soccer has brought people together. However, there has also been a dark side. Fans' intense passion for their national teams and club teams has occasionally led to violence. People causing this violence are often known as hooligans.

When Uruguay beat Argentina to win the 1930 World Cup, Argentineans attacked the Uruguayan embassy. Soccer violence was at its peak in the 1980s, especially in the United Kingdom. The problem grew so bad that English club teams were banned from international competition for a while.

Soccer continues to be a uniting influence among both young and old Ivorians—and around the world.

soccer players have been able to unite Ivorians like nothing else has.

Sport has long been known to unite people, whether they are players on a team or just fans. But no sport has had the global effect of soccer. Since the game began spreading in the mid-1800s, more people around the world have watched or played soccer than any other sport. To many of them, soccer is more than a game: it is a way of life.

CHAPTER 2

CREATING A GAME

K icking a ball. It's a pretty simple idea that dates back centuries. The Chinese were kicking a ball for sport as early as 200 to 300 BCE. Their game was called Tsu' Chu. It involved kicking a ball into a small hole in a net that was nine meters (29.5 ft) in the air.

Other similar games emerged around the world. People in Japan played Kemari around 400 CE. The game was similar to juggling a soccer ball today. A group of people stood in a circle. They tried to keep the ball in the air without using their hands. People in places such as Greece, Rome, South America, and Central America also played similar games throughout history. Although many of these games had some of the same ideas, they were all independent. And none of them was soccer as we know it today.

Ralph Squire played soccer for Cambridge University and the English national team during the late nineteenth century.

English Beginnings

The English were responsible for the development and growth of the sport that is so popular today. Ball games had been played in England since at least the twelfth century. But there were still no standard rules. In 1848, a group of students at Cambridge University in England wrote rules for soccer.

The students' rules did not stick. Yet the sport began to grow. Soon the first official soccer clubs formed. They began publishing their own rules as well. In 1863, the clubs were united. Leaders from 11 English soccer clubs came together to create the English Football Association (FA).

Association Football

The FA created rules for a game called association football. This name separated the sport from rugby. It was the official beginning of the sport now known as soccer.

Early soccer games were quite different from today's games. The use of hands was not outlawed until six years after the FA began. Modern concepts such as 11-person teams, goal kicks, and throw-ins were eventually added. As the FA grew, its rules became accepted throughout England. Soon Ireland, Scotland, and Wales had soccer associations, too.

The FA did much more than define the rules. As the sport grew, the need for a tournament arose. The FA Cup was created for the 1871–72 season. The FA organized the first international game between two countries in 1872. England and Scotland played to a 0–0 draw in Scotland. Beginning in 1885, the FA allowed players to be paid.

To this day, any professional or amateur team that is a member of the FA competes in the FA Cup. Similar cups exist in many countries. Some examples are the Copa del Rey in Spain and the US Open Cup in the United States.

In 1888 the Football League was created. It was the world's first professional soccer league. Today the Football League includes the 72 teams in England's second, third, and fourth divisions. England's first division, the Premier League, is separate.

EQUIPMENT

The first shin guards were worn in a soccer game in 1874. Today, shin guards, cleats, and a uniform are the only pieces of personal equipment needed to play an official soccer game. However, all you really need to play soccer is a ball. Many people play soccer barefoot, some by choice and others because they can't afford shoes. In 1950, India had to withdraw from the World Cup because the team did not have shoes.

Taking the World by Storm

Great Britain was very influential during the nineteenth century. Traveling British students, sailors, and other workers began teaching soccer to people around the world as early as the 1860s. Before long, people were playing the sport in countries throughout Europe, Africa, Asia, and North and South America. In 1904, seven European countries formed the Fédération Internationale de Football Association (FIFA). This organized the sport globally.

Club Teams

Today, new professional sports teams are usually expansion franchises. When a league decides to expand, a brand new franchise can join if it pays a large fee. The origins of many top soccer clubs from the late nineteenth century and early twentieth century were decidedly different.

SOCCER OR FOOTBALL

Association football is known by different names throughout the world. Most Americans, Canadians, and Australians call it soccer. But the majority of people in the world call the sport football. It is, after all, a game played with the feet. So why soccer? When association football was created, English college students took the "soc" from association and nicknamed the sport soccer. Soccer and football are interchangeable names for the sport in Britain.

West Bromwich Albion, an English club team, won the 1892 FA Cup 3–0 over Aston Villa. Both teams still exist today.

In England, many teams began through local companies. Manchester United is one of the most popular and successful club teams in the world. However, when workers from a railroad company founded the team in 1878, it was named Newton Heath. The club became Manchester United in 1902 when a local brewery bought it. Arsenal is another popular English team today. Arsenal began in 1886 when workers of a weapons factory founded it as an amateur team.

The English were also influential in forming club teams abroad. An Englishman founded the Milan Cricket and Football Club in 1899. It became Associazione Calcio (AC) Milan in 1938 and is one of the world's most famous teams today. However, AC Milan originally did not allow international players on its roster. So Football Club Internazionale Milano was formed as an alternative in 1908. Unlike its neighbor, it allowed foreign players. Today the famous club is known as Inter Milan.

Real Madrid in Spain is also one of the most famous club teams today. The team was founded in 1902 as Madrid Football Club. However, it became Real Madrid in 1920 when King Alfonso XIII blessed it. (Real is Spanish for royal.) Other teams were simply created by neighbors. Boca Juniors is one of the most famous club teams in Argentina today. Irishmen and Italian immigrants in the poor La Boca neighborhood of Buenos Aires founded it as an amateur team in 1905.

PROMOTION AND RELEGATION

Beginning in England in 1899, the teams that finished at the bottom of the standings were relegated to the next lowest division. Meanwhile, the teams that finished atop a lower division were promoted to the next highest division. Today there are 23 divisions, or tiers, in English soccer. Dozens of leagues make up those tiers. The EPL is the only league in the top tier. Some form of promotion and relegation is used in many countries' soccer leagues, including most in Europe and South America.

England won the first Olympic gold medal in soccer on home soil in 1908. The Olympic Games were held in London, England.

More Competitions

Men's soccer debuted in the 1908 Olympic Games in London, England. South American teams were unable to travel to Europe for the 1908 and 1912 Games. So, they created their own continental tournament. Today it is called Copa América.

European and South American teams, as well as the United States, began playing together at the Olympics in 1924. However, soccer's global growth eventually demanded a true world championship tournament. The demand became a reality when FIFA held the first World Cup in 1930.

CHAPTER 3

THE WORLD'S GAME

T oday there is no sporting competition like the World Cup. More than 200 countries from all corners of the globe attempt to qualify for the tournament. Every four years, the 32 qualifiers meet for approximately four weeks in the World Cup finals. Millions of fans watch the games at the stadiums. Billions more watch on television.

The first World Cup was a more modest attraction. It was held in the South American country of Uruguay. Forty-one countries had national soccer associations. But only 13 teams played in the first World Cup. They were from Argentina, Belgium, Bolivia, Brazil, Chile, France, Mexico, Paraguay, Peru, Romania, the United States, Uruguay, and Yugoslavia.

Jose Nasazzi, captain of Uruguay's national soccer team, helped lead his team to victory in the 1930 World Cup.

Some of the early games had as few as approximately 2,000 fans. But World Cup fever picked up as the tournament continued. It hit a peak when Uruguay faced neighboring Argentina in front of nearly 60,000 fans in the final. Uruguay won the back-and-forth game led by its star player, Héctor Castro. The forward scored the fourth goal in the 4–2 win.

The Cup Comes to Europe

The 1930 World Cup set the stage for what was to come. As more people began playing soccer around the world, the tournament continued to grow. In its early years, however, the World Cup was largely composed of teams from Europe and South America. Only one or two countries from other regions competed in each of the first three World Cups. Italy won the

BICYCLE KICK

The bicycle kick is one of the most exciting moves in sports. To do one, you jump like you are doing a backflip and then scissor kick the ball in the opposite direction while in the air.

The origins of the move are disputed. However, many consider Brazilian forward Leônidas da Silva to be the creator. Known as the "Rubber Man" and "Black Diamond," Leônidas played on Brazil's 1934 and 1938 World Cup squads. He scored 25 goals in 26 games for Brazil. He was one of the country's first superstars.

Italy's Enrique Guaita works to get past the Austrian goalie to score the winning goal in a semifinal game of the 1934 World Cup.

1934 World Cup at home and then won the 1938 World Cup in France. Soon after the 1938 World Cup, Europe was involved in World War II (1939–1945). For the warring countries, soccer was put on the backburner. Even the World Cup was put on hold. After the war, life slowly returned to normal for Europeans. The professional soccer leagues returned first. Finally, in 1950, the world was ready for the fourth World Cup.

The tournament returned to South America with Brazil as the host. Brazil and England were favored teams, but neither won

WHAT AN UPSET

Soccer fell behind football, baseball, and basketball in popularity for many years in the United States. The sport once thrived in the country. It was first played in the United States in 1866 under the rules developed in London in 1863. Many European immigrants kept the sport popular into the early twentieth century. There was even a professional league called the American Soccer League. However, interest slowly waned as people were drawn to other sports.

By 1950, few Americans even knew that 17 semi-professional US soccer players were in Brazil for the World Cup. And why should they have? Among the players were a mailman, a dishwasher, and a hearse driver. The team's second opponent, England, had some of the best players in the world. But in front of 10,151 fans, US midfielder Walter Bahr took a long shot that US forward Joe Gaetjens headed into the goal in the 37th minute. The 1–0 score held up. England went into the Cup with 3–1 odds of winning. US odds were 500–1.

the Cup. England was knocked out first. A team of amateurs from the United States upset the England Three Lions 1–0 in the first round. Many consider it to be the greatest upset in soccer history.

Brazil fared better. The team made it to the final to play Uruguay. It was an epic game in front of around 200,000 fans. The teams took a combined 30 shots, but Uruguay came from behind to win 2–1. Brazilians were devastated by the defeat.

Attack-Minded Soccer

The Magical Magyars from Hungary were the main story heading into the 1954 World Cup in Switzerland. The team had a 31-game unbeaten

At the 1950 World Cup, Uruguay defender Alcides Ghiggia, *center*, scored the goal that brought Uruguayan victory.

streak and a unique brand of attacking soccer. They appeared to be a lock to win. Hungary used a 4–2–4 lineup to score a Cup record of 27 goals in its five games. But the winner was again an underdog. West Germany overcame a 2–0 deficit in the first eight minutes to beat Hungry 3–2 in the final. It was the first World Cup to have some of its games broadcast on television.

The Magical Magyars' era of dominance was over. But Hungary's playing style was not soon forgotten. Brazil entered the 1958 World Cup in Sweden with a similar attack-minded 4–2–4 formation. The Brazilian players used speed, precision, and creativity to beat the competition and finally achieve a World Cup title. A 17-year-old named Edson Arantes do Nascimento scored two goals in Brazil's 5–2 victory over Sweden in the final game. Better known as Pelé, he would soon become soccer's first true global superstar.

FORMATIONS

Before a game, each team's manager must decide how many defenders, midfielders, and forwards the team will use. These combinations are called formations. Today, the most common formation is 4–4–2, which means there are four defenders, four midfielders, and two forwards. In the past, it was more common to see formations such as the 4–2–4 that Hungary and Brazil used during the 1950s. With more forwards, those formations led to more offensive soccer.

West Germany's Hans Schaefer, *right*, tries to get past Hungarian goalie Gyula Grosics during the 1954 World Cup final. West Germany defeated Hungary 3–2.

CHAPTER 4

GLOBAL SUPERSTARS

As soccer has grown, certain countries and regions have become known for certain playing styles. Italians are known for their methodic, defensive soccer. Americans are known for being very athletic. Germans are known for being very organized and efficient.

In Brazil, players and fans pride themselves on playing beautifully. This is known as *joga bonito*. Many words have been used to describe the Brazilian style: free-flowing, spontaneous, dazzling, flamboyant, and joyful. Beautiful soccer was at its prime during Brazil's run of success from the late 1950s through the early 1970s. And new advances in television allowed people around the world to see it firsthand.

Brazilian star Pelé, *right*, encapsulated joga bonito.

Joga Bonito

Brazilian superstar Pelé was often front and center. He was injured in the second game of the 1962 World Cup in Chile, but his teammate Garrincha was still healthy. Garrincha is not as well known today. But many considered him to be Pelé's equal at the time. He showed why in the 1962 Cup. He scored four goals in the tournament. Brazil beat Czechoslovakia 3–1 in the final.

Brazil never lost a game in which Garrincha and Pelé were in the lineup together. Their opponents at the 1966 World Cup had an answer for that. The free-flowing Brazilians were slowed by their opponents' vicious play. An injured Pelé missed Brazil's second game. Garrincha missed the third game. Both were losses, and Brazil went home early. On home soil, England won its only World Cup through 2010.

ANY SIZE

Soccer players come in all sizes. Take a look at the US men's national team that competed in the 2010 World Cup. Defender Steve Cherondolo was the smallest player at 5-foot-6 and 145 pounds. Fellow defender Oguchi Onyewu was the biggest at 6-foot-4 and 210 pounds. Goalies tend to be larger than field players. All three of the US goalies were 6-foot-3 or taller. Women's soccer players also vary. At the 2011 Women's World Cup, the US players ranged from 5-foot-4 to 5-foot-10.

Through 2011, Pelé held the world record with 1,281 career goals.

By the 1970 World Cup, Garrincha was gone and Pelé nearly was, too. He threatened to retire following the brutal play in 1966. But in the end, Pelé returned for his fourth and final World Cup. Many consider it to be the best one ever. Brazil played its joga bonito style of soccer all the way to the final. Defensive-minded Italy was no match for perhaps the greatest Brazil team ever. Pelé opened the scoring in the final. Brazil capped off a 4–1 rout with a famous goal in which eight of the 10 field players touched the ball on an end-to-end attack. It was Brazilian soccer at its finest.

Total Football

A Dutch club team called Ajax soon came out with a flashy, dynamic style of soccer. The Dutch called it "Total Football." Each of the 10 field players was able to switch positions on the fly. That allowed them to mount a lively attack. It required versatile and talented players.

Luckily for Ajax, they had just that in Johann Cruyff. He led the team to the European Cup title for three straight seasons beginning in 1970–71. Total Football soon spread to the national team, Oranje. Cruyff was the star for this team, too. Perhaps his most legendary move was the Cruyff Turn. He first used it to evade a Swedish defender during an international game. Cruyff

EUROPEAN CUP

Today the European Cup is called the Champions League. It pits all of the top club teams from Europe against each other in the continent's championship tournament. The European Cup was the first of its kind when it began in 1955–56. Today every continent has a Champions League or a similar tournament. It is called Copa Libertadores in South America.

Johann Cruyff led Holland to the final game in the 1974 World Cup.

pretended to pass the ball in one direction and then dragged the ball in the opposite direction behind him. The defender was sufficiently juked out.

The team known for its orange jerseys dazzled the fans at the 1974 World Cup in West Germany. The Dutch scored 14 goals and gave up just one in six games leading up to the final. However, a strong West German team finally overtook the Oranje in the final.

Total Football produced some of the most exciting teams and matches of the 1970s. But following the 2010 World Cup, Holland was still trying to drop its runner-up title. The Oranje finished as World Cup runners-up for the third time in 2010.

Platini and Maradona

Live television helped make the world's game even more accessible by the 1980s. That helped introduce the world to more vibrant soccer superstars. The early 1980s were France midfielder Michel Platini's time to shine. His creativity and ability to score from midfield helped France win the 1984 European Championship. He also thrived for his club teams, notably Italian club Juventus. Platini and France were never able to get past the semifinals of the World Cup, though.

SOCCER FEVER

Soccer was barely on the radar in the United States when the North American Soccer League (NASL) debuted in 1968. Pelé changed that when he came out of retirement to sign with the New York Cosmos in 1975. Stadiums filled up to watch him play. The once-forgotten sport was re-introduced to a new generation of US fans.

Several other older European stars came to play in the NASL, too. Among them were Johann Cruyff, Franz Beckenbauer, Eusebio, and Bobby Moore.

In 1985, the NASL folded. The league left a legacy, though. Several current US teams brought old NASL nicknames back to life. Most importantly, the league helped create many new soccer fans.

DER KAISER

Germany's Franz Beckenbauer was known as "der Kaiser," meaning "the Emperor." He played in three World Cups for West Germany, helping Die Mannschaft, as the team is called, win the title in 1974. He also starred for German club team Bayern Munich. Beckenbauer revolutionized the sweeper position. This refers to a central defender who plays behind the team's other defenders. He was the leader of the defense. Yet he was also a lethal scorer when going up on the attack. Many consider him to be among the top players to ever play the game. Beckenbauer also won the World Cup as a manager with West Germany in 1990.

Argentina stepped up in a big way in 1986. A 17-year-old Diego Maradona had been a late scratch from Argentina's 1978 World Cup–winning team. This was followed by a forgettable performance in his first World Cup in 1982. He was sent off with a red card as Argentina went out in the second round. But when Maradona was on top of his game, he was nearly unstoppable. The 1986 World Cup in Mexico was one of those times.

The center forward was only 5-foot-5. But his ball skills and field awareness made him a terror to defend. Millions watched on television as he dominated the 1986 World Cup from start to finish. In one quarterfinal game against England, Maradona scored what might be the most controversial *and* best goal in World Cup history.

Maradona's first goal is now known as the Hand of God goal. He appeared to head the ball past England's goalie. However, Maradona later revealed that he had hit the ball with his hand. He called the goal "a little of the hand of god and a little of the head of Maradona." Four minutes after his first goal, Maradona collected the ball inside his half of the field. Then he dribbled the length of the field, passing five England players, and scored. It is known as the Goal of the Century.

Maradona eventually led Argentina to the title in an exciting final against West Germany. Argentina's Jorge Burruchaga scored the game-winning goal in the 84th minute as his team won 3–2. That proved to be the high point of Maradona's brilliant career.

The 1990 World Cup was known for its negative and violent play. Maradona was able to again lead Argentina to the final. But in a rematch of the 1986 final, West Germany beat Argentina in a defensive-minded game.

THE CARDS

Soccer is famous for its two small cards: the yellow card and the red card. A yellow card shown to a player is a warning. If the player receives two yellow cards in one game, or if he or she commits a particularly bad foul, he or she is shown a red card and is ejected from the game. The cards were first used at the 1970 World Cup. The first World Cup red card was handed out in 1974.

Diego Maradona is lifted into the air with the trophy after leading Argentina to the 1986 World Cup title in Mexico.

The years that followed saw Maradona struggle with drugs, obesity, and ties to organized crime. He even missed part of the 1994 World Cup due to a positive drug test. Maradona retired from playing in 1997. Despite the controversies surrounding Maradona's life, he remained a hero in Argentina. He was even named the national team's head coach for the 2010 World Cup, where he led Argentina to the quarterfinals.

CHAPTER 5

SPREADING THROUGHOUT THE UNITED STATES

O n November 19, 1989, Paul Caligiuri scored what many consider to be the most important goal in US soccer history. His left-footed strike from approximately 25 yards (22.86 m) was enough to beat host Trinidad and Tobago 1–0. More importantly, it sent the United States to its first World Cup in 40 years.

The 1990 World Cup in Italy was not a great success for the United States. The team lost all three of its games. Still, the country had seen soccer fall into the background for several decades. Just getting there was a major step forward. The 1990 World Cup was the first of three major events that helped bring back soccer's popularity in the United States during the 1990s.

US defender Paul Caligiuri, *left*, scored the game-winning goal that led the United States to the 1990 World Cup.

World Cup Hosts

In 1988, FIFA voted to hold the 1994 World Cup in the United States. Some people, both inside and outside the country, disagreed with the decision. They believed a country that was more enthusiastic about the sport should hold the World Cup. Some believed the United States might not have even qualified had it not gotten an automatic berth as the host.

But that did not deter the US team. Led by striker Eric Wynalda, midfielder Tab Ramos, and others, the team got off to a surprise start. The Yanks, as the US team is known, tied Switzerland 1–1 in their first game. Then they beat Colombia—a team that some thought might win the entire Cup—2–1 in their second game. More than 90,000 fans watched the victory at the Rose Bowl in Southern California. Although the Yanks lost to Romania in their next game, they advanced to the second round.

WORLD CUP SUCCESS

Some soccer officials worried about how people in the United States would react to the 1994 World Cup. But they didn't have to. Soccer was relatively new to most Americans. Still, approximately 3.6 million people attended the games. That was more than 1 million beyond the previous record set at the 1990 World Cup. The World Cup added 12 more games beginning in 1998. But the 1994 total attendance and average attendance records still stand following the 2010 Cup.

Alexi Lalas, easily recognizable with his red hair and goatee, celebrates after the United States beat Colombia in the 1994 World Cup.

However, Brazil ended the Yanks' tournament in the next game and soon became champion.

A New League

After the first round of the 1994 World Cup, a *Sports Illustrated* reporter had a prediction. "The enthusiasm generated by the [US] win over Colombia figures to have a long-lasting effect in the US," he wrote. Indeed it did. In 1996, Major League

The excitement surrounding the US team at the 1994 World Cup was helped by some of the team's quirky characters. Defender Alexi Lalas and midfielder Cobi Jones became the most recognizable faces of the team. Lalas was known for his long, curly, red hair and goatee. Jones was known for his dreadlocks. The two players were featured on the cover of a 1994 *Sports Illustrated for Kids* magazine with the title "Soccer Madness."

Soccer (MLS) debuted with 10 teams. It was the first major professional soccer league in the United States since the NASL ended in the 1980s. Many of the top US stars played in MLS's first season in 1996. Future Yanks' legend Brian McBride was the first player chosen in the league's first draft. Other US stars such as Cobi Jones, Alexi Lalas, Eddie Pope, and Wynalda played in MLS during its early years.

However, the enthusiasm did not result in wins at the 1998 World Cup in France. In fact, the United States finished last out of 32 teams at the tournament. It was a disappointing Cup for the country. But, the 1990s greatly increased interest and participation in soccer within the United States.

Women Take Over

Women had been documented playing soccer as early as 1895. However, women's soccer had either been banned or largely ignored in most countries for the next several decades. That finally began to change in the 1970s.

US women have long been leaders in the sport. Many attribute that to Title IX. That 1972 legislation required US schools and colleges to offer equal opportunities to men and women in sports and other areas. Women's college soccer began taking off soon after that. By 1985, enough women were playing to create the US women's national team. Very few countries had women's national soccer teams at the time.

Michelle Akers was called to the US national team in 1985. She played on the team for 15 years. Many consider her to be the greatest women's soccer player of all time. Five teenagers joined Akers on the national team in 1987 and 1988. They were Brandi Chastain, Joy Fawcett, Julie Foudy, Kristine Lilly, and Mia Hamm. Those players would become known as the "Fab Five." They starred for the United States for more than a decade together.

DID YOU KNOW?

No World Cup game had been held indoors until the United States played Switzerland at the Pontiac Silverdome near Detroit, Michigan, on June 18, 1994. A special natural grass surface was installed in the stadium for the game. Four first-round matches took place at the Silverdome.

By 1991, there was enough global interest to host the first Women's World Cup. The United States won the 1991 Women's World Cup as well as the first Olympic women's soccer tournament in 1996. The team's games occasionally attracted large crowds. More than 76,000 were on hand for the gold-medal game in 1996. But few could have anticipated the magic that occurred when the United States hosted the 1999 Women's World Cup.

1999 World Cup

It began when 78,972 fans showed up for the United States' opening game against Denmark. Suddenly, the country—women and men—began to take notice of women's soccer in a big way. Led by talented players such as Hamm, a forward, and Akers, a midfielder, the team had likeable athletes and was exciting to watch. The crowds continued to be large as the US squad cruised

MIA HAMM

Legendary US forward Mia Hamm did not particularly enjoy being in the spotlight. It was hard to avoid it for a player of her caliber and natural charisma, though. During her long career, Hamm played in four Women's World Cups and three Olympic Games for the United States. She ended her career in 2004 with two Women's World Cup titles and two Olympic gold medals. No woman in the world has matched Hamm's 158 career goals and 144 assists.

Forward Mia Hamm helped lead the United States to two Women's World Cup titles and two Olympic gold medals.

to the finals. When the United States met China in the final game, 90,185 fans and more than 500 reporters showed up at the Rose Bowl. Among the fans was US President Bill Clinton.

Few sporting events have captivated the nation like the final of the 1999 Women's World Cup. An estimated 40 million people worldwide saw it on television. The offensive-minded Chinese team could not get past the defensive-minded Americans. After 90 minutes of regular time and 30 minutes of extra time, the score remained tied at 0–0. It all came down to penalty kicks.

The shootout was close, too. The first four US shooters scored. However, one of the Chinese shooters had missed. US defender Chastain stepped forward with the game in her hands. All she had to do was score and the United States would win the title. And she did. Chastain buried her shot into the back right corner of the net. She then pulled her jersey off and fell to her knees in celebration. Her image was splashed across the front of the next *Sports Illustrated* with the simple headline: "Yes!"

The 1990s were a turning point for soccer in the United States. Soccer had emerged as a major team sport after many years in the background. The US men were slowly but surely working to catch up to their competition. The US women were leaders in the growing sport. And millions of US youth were now playing soccer.

Brandi Chastain's iconic celebratory moment after she made the game-winning goal in the 1999 Women's World Cup

CHAPTER 6

TO NEW HEIGHTS

Technology has given fans greater access to their favorite players and teams. Games that were once only available to locals are now available to the masses on satellite television or the Internet. Meanwhile, news about players is also widely available online. These factors have helped soccer's popularity expand even more into the twenty-first century.

Going Global

Soccer showed its global expansion in 2002. The World Cup that year was held in South Korea and Japan. It marked the first time the tournament was held in Asia. During the Cup, several emerging soccer nations surprised the old guard with their strong play.

Spanish fans watch the 2010 World Cup at a public square in Canada. New technology has made watching faraway soccer games easier than ever.

Senegal beat defending champions France 1–0 in the opening match and advanced to the second round. Led by midfielder Claudio Reyna, forward Brian McBride, and goalie Brad Friedel, the United States advanced to the quarterfinals. South Korea became the first Asian team to reach the semifinals and eventually finished fourth behind Turkey. In the end, traditional power Brazil beat Germany 2–0 in the final. But the 2002 World Cup was a wake-up call for the world's best teams.

Women's Growth

The 1999 Women's World Cup showed that women's soccer could be a big-time sport. As other nations improved, the tournaments became more competitive. Germany defeated Sweden 2–1 to win the 2003 Women's World Cup. Germany then beat Brazil to win

TOURNAMENTS

Professional sports teams in the United States generally have a regular season and a postseason, with the postseason winner being declared the champion. Soccer has a more complex system. In soccer, the winner of the regular season is declared the league champion. Meanwhile, the teams also play in independent tournaments that run simultaneously to the regular season. For example, the European Champions League pits the top European teams against each other and the FA Cup pits every English team against each other. To make that work, most regular-season games are scheduled for the weekend while tournament games take place mid-week. Tournaments among national teams usually take place during the professional leagues' off-seasons.

the 2007 event. The United States finished in third place both times.

The look of the US women's national team began to change around 2004. The United States won the Olympic gold medal that year. But soon many of the stars that captivated the nation in 1999 began to retire. Among them were Joy Fawcett, Julia Foudy, and Mia Hamm.

A new generation of international stars emerged to take their place. Among them were Germany striker Birgit Prinz, Brazil striker Marta Vieira da Silva, and US striker Abby Wambach. But women's soccer has hit a few bumps since 1999. The first US professional women's league debuted in 2001 but folded in 2003. However, a new US pro league called Women's Professional Soccer (WPS) was formed in 2007.

MARTA

Brazil has long been known for its creative strikers, from Pelé to Romario to Ronaldo. Now it can add Marta to that list. Marta Vieira da Silva burst onto the scene at the 2002 Under-19 World Championship. She soon led Brazil to become a power in women's soccer. The team won silver medals at the 2004 and 2008 Olympics as well as the 2007 Women's World Cup. Since 2009, Marta has played professionally for various teams in the WPS in the United States. She won her fifth consecutive FIFA Player of the Year Award in 2010.

Portuguese star Cristiano Ronaldo, of Real Madrid, dribbles away from Barcelona's Lionel Messi, of Argentina, in a 2011 Champions League game.

Champions League

Today, most of the world's top male players play professionally in Europe. When the top European club teams meet in the Champions League, the games tend to be very exciting. The Champions League helped establish David Beckham's stardom when his Manchester United team won it in 1999. Many other top players have become international superstars through the Champions League since then.

One of the most dominant teams of the early 2000s was FC Barcelona. Brazil and Barcelona forward Ronaldinho became a global superstar in helping Barcelona win the 2006 Champions League. Ace striker Lionel Messi of Argentina was the star as Barcelona won it again in 2009 and 2011. The stars of 2008 champions Manchester United were England forward Wayne Rooney and Portugal winger Cristiano Ronaldo. Messi, Rooney, and Ronaldo also starred in the 2006 and 2010 World Cups.

Major Step

Soccer took a major step in 2010 when the World Cup was held in South Africa. It was the first time the tournament was held in Africa. The African nations did not do as well as many

DAVID BECKHAM

David Beckham is known as a great player, with his signature skill being his bending free kicks. But few would argue he is the greatest player to ever live. Still, he might be the most famous soccer player in history. The midfielder has model-like good looks and a pop star wife. He is a fashion icon off the field and a superb passer on it. And as a key player for two of the most famous teams in the world in the late 1990s, Manchester United and England, Beckham became a global icon. In 2003, Beckham moved to another of the world's biggest teams, Real Madrid. Such was the excitement that his physical examination was broadcast on pay-per-view television in Spain. He has played for the Los Angeles Galaxy in MLS since 2007.

hoped. Only Ghana reached the quarterfinals. Spain won the World Cup for the first time. But the tournament showcased a continent that could be a future leader in the sport.

Soccer's global momentum continued at the 2011 Women's World Cup. US fan interest boomed after the United States defeated Brazil in a dramatic quarterfinal game. The US squad entered overtime with 10 players due to a red card. Then Brazil took the lead. However, Wambach headed the ball into Brazil's net in the 122nd minute to tie it up. The United States eventually won in a shootout. After defeating France in the semifinals, the United States reached the final for the first time since 1999.

The tournament also saw many new countries shine. None shined more than Japan. It reached the final by defeating powerhouse Germany—the tournament's host—and a strong Sweden team. Then Japan came back twice against the United

LANDON DONOVAN

Midfielder Landon Donovan began his career with Bayer Leverkusen in Germany. However, he emerged into a star with the San Jose Earthquakes and the Los Angeles Galaxy in MLS. Through 2010, Donovan was named the US Player of the Year seven times. Donovan also played in the 2002, 2006, and 2010 World Cups for the United States. He is the all-time leading scorer in US national team history. His five goals in the World Cup also lead all US players.

Japan became the first Asian country to win the Women's World Cup when it defeated the United States in the 2011 final.

States in the final before winning in a shootout. That made Japan the first Asian country to win the Women's World Cup.

The 2010 World Cup and 2011 Women's World Cup were previews of things to come. FIFA plans to bring the World Cup to new parts of the world. Meanwhile, the 2015 Women's World Cup will expand from 16 to 24 teams. People have been kicking balls for thousands of years. With more people playing and watching soccer than ever before, there is no end in sight for the beautiful game.

TIMELINE

1848 — Students at Cambridge University in England write the first rules of the sport that is now known as soccer.

1863 — Eleven English club soccer teams meet and create the English FA. The FA eventually standardizes the rules to association football and creates the FA Cup and the Football League.

1904 — Seven European nations form FIFA to organize global soccer.

1908 — Men's soccer is competed in as a medal event in the Olympic Games for the first time.

1916 — The first official South American championships take place. Today the tournament is known as Copa América.

1930 — Uruguay defeats Argentina to win the first FIFA World Cup. The United States finishes third of the 13 teams, its best-ever finish.

1939 — Soccer either shuts down or is pared down in many parts of the world as World War II begins.

1950 — A US team made up of mostly amateurs upsets England 1–0 in one of the greatest upsets in World Cup history. Uruguay shocks Brazil to win its second World Cup.

1970 — In what many consider to be the best World Cup, Brazil's Pelé leads Brazil to its third title. Red and yellow cards are used for the first time in a World Cup.

1973 — Behind star Johann Cruyff, Dutch club Ajax wins its third straight European Cup by using its Total Football approach. The Dutch national team would adopt this approach but was unable to win a World Cup title.

1986
In a World Cup quarterfinal game against England, Argentina's Diego Maradona scores the controversial Hand of God goal and then the magnificent Goal of the Century. He eventually led Argentina to its second title.

1989
Paul Caligiuri scores on a long shot to beat Trinidad and Tobago 1–0. The win secures the United States' first World Cup berth in 40 years.

1994
The United States upsets Colombia in the first round of the World Cup on home soil and advances to the second round. Brazil defeats Italy in the first final decided by a penalty shootout.

1996
The US women's national team wins the first Olympic gold medal in women's soccer in Atlanta, Georgia. MLS debuts.

1999
In front of 90,185 fans at the Rose Bowl, the US women's national team defeats China in a shootout to win the Women's World Cup.

2002
The World Cup is held in Asia for the first time when Japan and Korea co-host it. Several surprise teams make runs in the tournament, but Brazil eventually adds its record fifth title in a win over Germany.

2004
After winning a gold medal at the Olympic Games, legendary US women's soccer players Joy Fawcett, Julia Foudy, and Mia Hamm retire.

2009
A new women's professional league, WPS, debuts in the United States. Among the stars are Abby Wambach and Marta.

2010
The World Cup is held in Africa for the first time when South Africa hosts. Spain defeats the Netherlands in the final.

2011
Japan beats the United States in a shootout to become the first Asian country to win the Women's World Cup.

MEN

Franz Beckenbauer
West Germany

David Beckham
England

George Best
Northern Ireland

Bobby Charlton
England

Johann Cruyff
Netherlands

Alfredo Di Stefano
Argentina

Didier Drogba
Ivory Coast

Eusebio
Portugal

Diego Maradona
Argentina

Lionel Messi
Argentina

Pelé
Brazil

Michel Platini
France

Ferenc Puskas
Hungary

Ronaldinho
Brazil

Ronaldo
Brazil

Lev Yashin
Russia

Zinedane Zidane
France

Dino Zoff
Italy

WOMEN

Michelle Akers
United States

Mia Hamm
United States

Marta
Brazil

Birgit Prinz
Germany

Hope Solo
United States

Abby Wambach
United States

assist
A pass that leads directly to a goal.

berth
An entry into something.

creativity
The ability to play in new and imaginative ways.

formation
The arrangement of players and positions on the field.

hooligans
Fans who commit violence at or around soccer games.

injury time
Following the 45 minutes in each half in a soccer game, added time as determined by the referee to account for stoppages in play.

joga bonito
A Brazilian style of soccer that means playing beautifully.

juggling
Keeping a soccer ball in the air using feet, knees, chest, and head.

precision
The ability to have a high degree of accuracy.

promotion
When a team finishes at or near the top of the league standings and is sent to a higher division.

relegation
When a team finishes at or near the bottom of the league standings and is sent to a lower division.

shootout
The part of a competition that decides the winner after extra time still leaves a tie score.

substitution
When one player replaces a teammate during a soccer game. Each team is allowed three per game on the top levels.

underdog
A competitor who is not expected to win.

Selected Bibliography

Hirshey, David, and Roger Bennett. *The ESPN World Cup Companion*. New York: Ballantine, 2010. Print.

Hunt, Chris, ed. *The Complete Book of Soccer*. Buffalo, NY: Firefly, 2006. Print.

Radnedge, Keir. *The Complete Encyclopedia of Soccer*. London: Carlton, 2006. Print.

Further Readings

Drogba, Didier. *Didier Drogba: The Autobiography*. London: Aurum, 2008. Print.

Longman, Jere. *The Girls of Summer*. New York: HarperCollins, 2000. Print.

Wahl, Grant. *The Beckham Experiment*. New York: Crown, 2009. Print.

Web Links

To learn more about soccer, visit ABDO Publishing Company online at **www.abdopublishing.com**. Web sites about soccer are featured on our Book Links page. These links are routinely monitored and updated to provide the most current information available.

Places to Visit

Home Depot Center

18400 Avalon Blvd.
Carson, CA 90746
(310) 630-2000
www.homedepotcenter.com
One of the first soccer-specific stadiums in the United States, the Home Depot Center is the home field for MLS teams Chivas USA and the Los Angeles Galaxy. The 27,000-seat stadium is also the training headquarters for the US men's and women's national teams.

National Sports Center

1700 105th Ave. NE
Blaine, MN 55449
(800) 535-4730
www.nscsports.org
With 48 fields, the National Sports Center is recognized as the largest soccer complex in the world. Several youth soccer games and tournaments take place here each year, notably the USA Cup, which is considered the largest youth soccer tournament in the western hemisphere.

About the Author

Chrös McDougall is a sportswriter and author based in Minnesota's Twin Cities. He covers Olympic sports for the US Olympic Committee's Web site, TeamUSA.org, and has written several books on sports. After a youth soccer career, he covered English soccer while working at the Associated Press bureau in London in 2007. McDougall lives in St. Paul with his wife.